P9-CCK-331

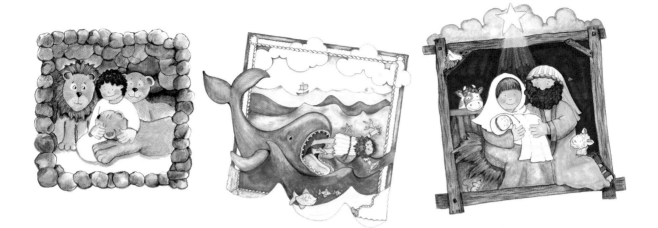

Presented to

_____

From

_____

Date

_____

GOD IS GREAT

A Toddler's Bible Storybook

Carolyn Larsen & Illustrations by Caron Turk

God Is Great

Copyright © 2011 Educational Publishing Concepts, Inc.

Published by Crossway
            1300 Crescent Street
            Wheaton, Illinois 60187

All rights reserved. No part of this publication may be reproduced, stored in a retrieval system, or transmitted in any form by any means, electronic, mechanical, photocopy, recording, or otherwise, without the prior permission of the publisher, except as provided for by USA copyright law.

Cover design: Amy Bristow

Cover illustration: Caron Turk

First printing 2011

Printed in China

Hardback ISBN: 978-1-4335-1559-0

PDF ISBN: 978-1-4335-2507-0

Mobipocket ISBN: 978-1-4335-2508-7

Library of Congress Cataloging-in-Publication Data

Larsen, Carolyn, 1950–
 God is great: a toddler's Bible storybook / Carolyn Larsen.
    p. cm.
 ISBN-13: 978-1-4335-1559-0 (hc)
 1. Bible stories, English. 2. God (Christianity) — Juvenile literature. I. Title.

BS551.3.L36 2010
220.9'505--dc22   2010022866

Crossway is a publishing ministry of Good News Publishers.

OGP   17   16   15   14   13   12   11

15 14 13 12 11 10 9 8 7 6 5 4 3 2 1

GOD IS GREAT

A Toddler's Bible Storybook

Carolyn Larsen & Illustrations by Caron Turk

:: CROSSWAY WHEATON, ILLINOIS

Contents

God Makes Everything

Genesis 1–2

God was here before anything else.

There were no people, no plants, no animals, no earth.

God said, "Let there be light," and light came.

He said, "Let there be plants and trees and rivers."

God said, "Let there be puppies and giraffes and butterflies."

God made Adam and Eve, the first people, too.

God made everything, everything there is!

But remember, God was the first thing here!

God was here in the beginning!

God Starts Over

Genesis 6:1–9:17

People stopped obeying God.

They did mean and selfish things.

That is called sin. God hates sin.

God decided to start over.

He sent a big flood that covered everything on the whole earth.

But there was one man who still obeyed God.

His name was Noah.

God kept Noah and his family safe from the flood.

They stayed in a big boat with lots of animals.

"Thank you, God!" Noah said.

God hates sin.

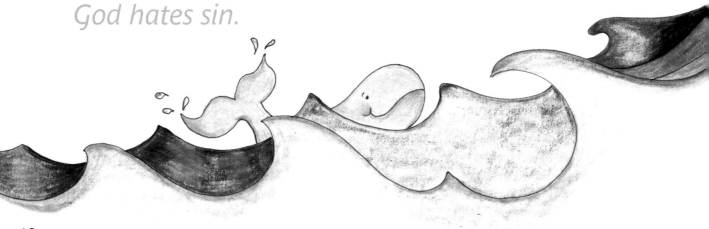

God Saves Joseph

Genesis 37–46

Jacob had 12 sons.

Joseph was the second youngest. He was his father's favorite son.

Joseph's brothers were jealous of him. They wanted him to go away.

His brothers sold Joseph to be a slave in Egypt.

But God had a different plan for Joseph.

He made Joseph a very important ruler in Egypt.

Joseph forgave his brothers.

He even saved them when they needed help.

God's plan always happens.

God Watches over Moses

Exodus 2:1–10

"No more Hebrew baby boys!" an angry king said.

He ordered that all baby boys be killed.

"Not my baby!" one momma said.

"God has important things for him to do."

She put her baby in a basket and floated it down the river.

"Please protect him, God," she prayed.

God did! A princess found baby Moses.

She took him home and raised him as her son!

God protects his children.

God Gives the Ten Commandments

Exodus 20:1–21

"Moses, meet me at the top of the mountain," God said.

"I will give you some important rules.

They will teach the people the best way to live.

These rules will show them how to treat others.

They will help them know how to serve me."

God wrote the rules on stone tablets. Moses took them to the people.

The rules are called the Ten Commandments.

God guides us in how to live.

God Makes the Walls Fall Down

Joshua 6

"I will give you this city," God told Joshua.
But there was a big wall around the city.
Guards stood on top of the wall.
How would Joshua get inside?
"March around the city with all your people and
blow your trumpets," God said. Joshua obeyed.
God made the big wall fall down. He gave the city to Joshua.

God keeps his promises!

19

God Helps Samson

Judges 13–16

Samson was the strongest man in the world.

He loved and served God, too.

But Samson made some bad choices.

He did some bad things.

Samson was captured by God's enemies, the Philistines.

"Help me one more time!" Samson prayed.

God did!

He helped Samson beat the Philistines all by himself!

God gives second chances.

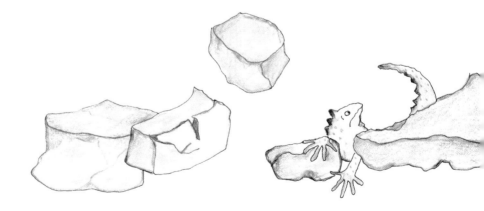

God Strengthens David

1 Samuel 17:1–51

Can a young boy defeat a giant soldier?
He can if God helps him!
David was a young boy.
Goliath was a giant soldier.
Goliath said bad things about God.
King Saul's soldiers were scared to fight the giant.
But little David was brave. He had a sling and 5 stones.
Goliath had a sword, spear, and shield.
But David won! God was on David's side!

Nothing is too hard for God!

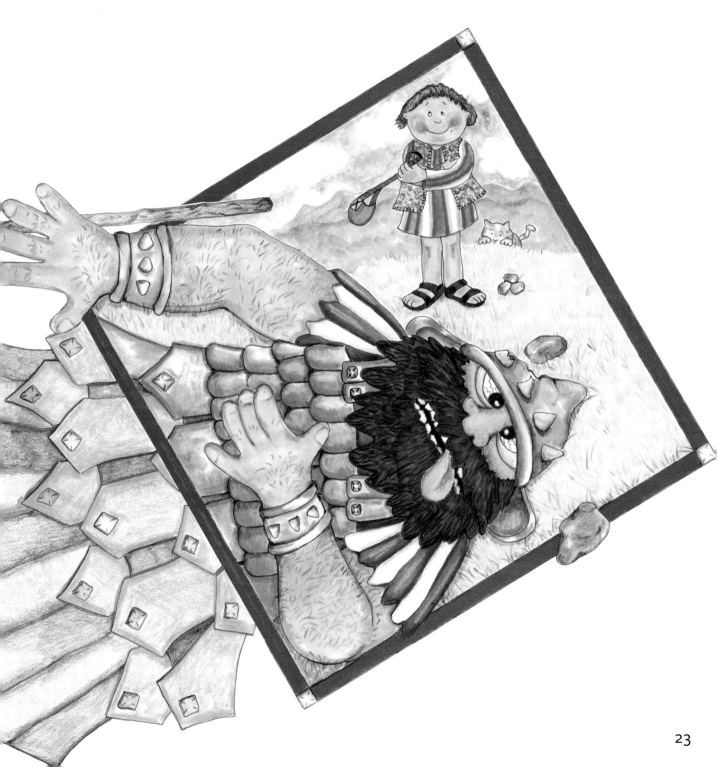

God Uses Esther

The Book of Esther

"Esther is my new queen," the king said.

No one knew that she was Jewish.

Haman was a mean man who worked for the king.

He wanted to hurt the Jews.

"How can I help my people?" Esther wondered.

She invited the king and Haman to a special dinner.

After dinner the king asked, "How can I thank you?"

"Save my people. Haman wants to hurt us!" Esther said.

"I will save you!" the king said.

God uses people.

God Protects Daniel

Daniel 6

Some men tricked the king into making a new law.

The law said no one could pray to God.

The men knew Daniel would break the law.

They were right. Daniel loved God very much.

He would pray to God no matter what.

Daniel was put into a den full of hungry lions.

That was the punishment for breaking the law.

But God protected Daniel. He kept the lions from hurting him.

God's power is over all!

God Teaches Jonah

Jonah 1–3

"Tell the people in Nineveh that I love them," God told Jonah.

"No," Jonah said. He hid on a boat. God knew where Jonah was.

He sent a big storm. The sailors were scared.

"Throw me overboard and the storm will stop," Jonah said.

They did and a big fish swallowed him.

For 3 days Jonah thought about how he disobeyed God.

"Give me another chance to obey," he prayed.

The fish spit Jonah out and he hurried to Nineveh.

God is patient.

28

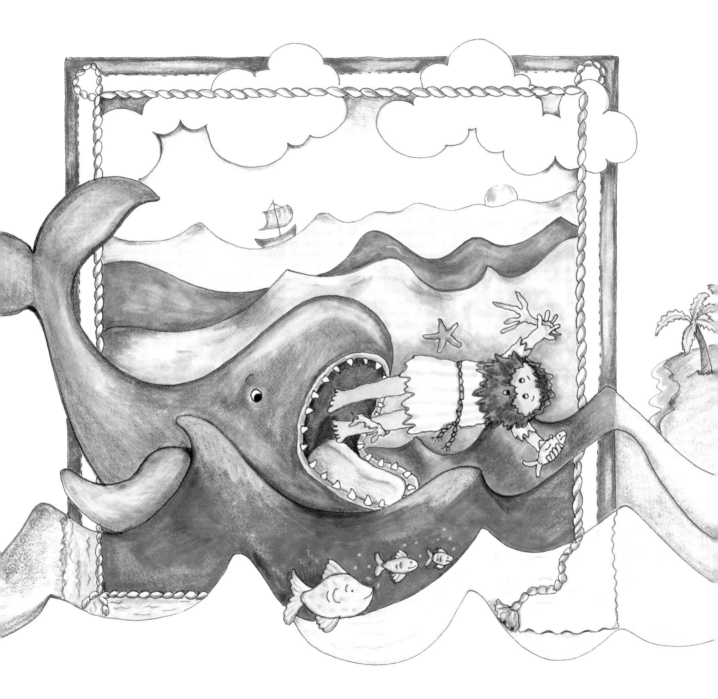

29

God's Best Gift

Luke 2:1-20

See baby Jesus sleeping in his mother's arms?
His mother wrapped him in cloth and laid him in the manger.
Angels told the shepherds that Jesus was born.
The shepherds hurried to Bethlehem to see him.
Jesus is God's very own Son.
God sent Jesus from heaven to live on earth.
He sent Jesus because he loves you very much.
Believing that Jesus is God's Son
is the only way to know God!

God's gift of love is Jesus.

Jesus Feeds 5,000

Matthew 14:13–21; Mark 6:32–44; Luke 9:10–17; John 6:1–13

One day many people came to hear Jesus teach.

Jesus' friends said, "It's dinner time. Send the people home."

But Jesus said, "You give them food."

But they didn't have any food.

What would they do?

"You can have my lunch," a little boy said.

It was 5 loaves of bread and 2 fish.

Jesus thanked God and broke the bread and fish into pieces.

5,000 people ate all they wanted.

God cares about our needs.

Jesus Teaches a Lesson

Luke 10:25–37

Jesus told this story:

Some robbers hurt a Jewish man.

They took his clothes and money and left him on the road.

A church worker came by. He didn't help the man.

Another church worker came. He didn't help either.

A man from the country of Samaria came by.

People from his country didn't like Jewish people.

But he helped the hurt man anyway.

People who love God should be kind to others like the Good Samaritan was.

God is love.

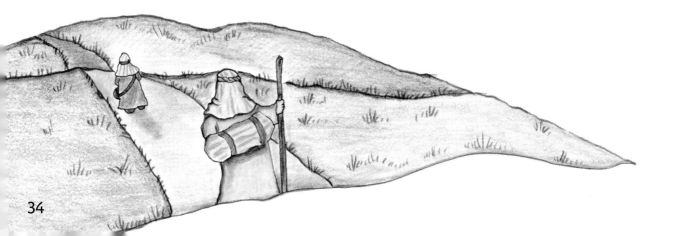

Jesus Walks on Water

Matthew 14:22–33; Mark 6:45–51; John 6:16–21

Jesus' friends were in a boat. A terrible storm came.

Jesus knew they were in trouble.

He walked on top of the water to reach them.

His friends saw a man walking on the water and were scared.

They didn't know it was Jesus.

Peter said, "Let me walk on water, too!"

"Come on," Jesus said.

Peter stepped onto the water, but he got scared and sank.

Jesus saved Peter and got in the boat.

Then he told the storm to stop.

God is always with you.

Jesus Dies, but Not Forever

Matthew 27:45–28:15; Mark 15:33–16:8; Luke 23:26–24:12; John 19:16–21

Jesus died on the cross.

Some bad people put him there.

Jesus let them do it because he loves all people.

He took our punishment for the bad things we do.

Jesus' friends buried him.

But the story wasn't over.

God brought Jesus back to life!

God is more powerful than anything else, even death!

God has victory over death!

Jesus Gives Us a Job

Matthew 28:19–20

"I know you love me," Jesus told his friends.
"Now I'm asking you to do something for me.
I want everyone everywhere to know that I love them.
So please tell people that I care.
Teach them to read the Bible so they can obey me.
This is very important work. You can't do it without my help.
I promise to be with you all the time. I promise to give you strength."

God gives us strength!